What fun is in store for you today! This RECORDER FUN SONGBOOK will have you playing the recorder quickly and easily while you learn to play some of your favorite children's songs.

CONTENTS

SONGS:

HAL•LEONARD®
CORPORATION
7777 W. BLUEMOUND RD. P.O. BOX 13819 MILWAUKEE, WI 53213

GETTING STARTED

HOLDING THE RECORDER

Here is how to hold the recorder. The mouthpiece rests on your lower lip, just like a drinking straw, with only a little of it actually going inside your mouth. Be sure that all of the finger holes line up on the front of the recorder as shown in the picture.

LEFT HAND — The first three fingers of your left hand (the little finger is not used) play the *top* three holes on the front of the recorder. The thumb of your left hand plays the hole on the back.

RIGHT HAND — The *bottom* four holes are played by your right-hand fingers. There is no hole for your right-hand thumb to play so it can help hold the recorder steady while the other fingers are busy playing.

Cover the top three holes with your left-hand fingers and the bottom four holes with your right-hand fingers. The thumb of your left hand covers the hole in the back of your recorder.

MAKING A SOUND

To make a sound on the recorder blow gently into the small opening at the top of the mouthpiece. You can change this sound by covering different holes with your thumb and fingers. For example, when you cover all of the thumb and finger holes you will get a low, quiet sound. When only one or two holes are covered the sound will be higher and much louder.

Here are some tips for getting the best possible sound out of your recorder:

Always blow gently into the mouthpiece — Breathe in and then gently blow into the mouthpiece as if you were sighing or using a straw to blow out a candle. Remember, always blow gently.

Leaks cause squeaks — Play the holes using the pads of your fingers and thumb (not the tips). Press against each hole firmly so that it is completely covered and no air can sneak out. Even a tiny leak of air will change a beautiful tone into a sudden squeak!

Use your tongue to start each tone — Place your tongue against the roof of your mouth just behind your front teeth and start each tone that you play by tonguing the syllable "du" or "too" as you blow gently into the recorder.

PLAYING A TONE

Musical sounds are called *tones*. Every tone has a letter name. *Finger charts* are used to show you exactly which holes should be covered in order to play a particular tone. Each circle on these charts represents one of the holes on your recorder. The thumb hole is represented by the circle to the left of the recorder in the chart.

●   means that you should cover that hole.

○   means that that hole should not be covered but left open.

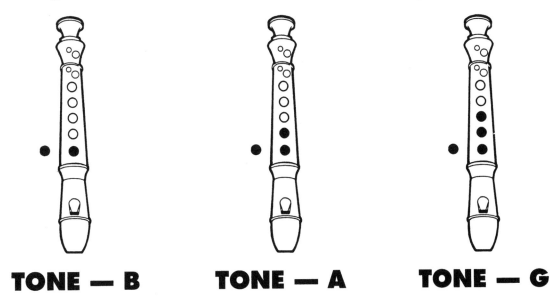

TONE — B   **TONE — A**   **TONE — G**

Use these three tones to play "Mary Had A Little Lamb:"

MARY HAD A LITTLE LAMB

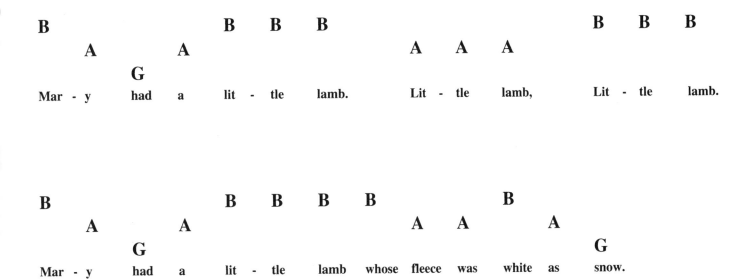

READING MUSIC

Musical notes are an easy way to see everything that you need to know in order to play a song on your recorder:

How high or low — Notes are written on five lines that are called a *staff*. The higher a note is written on the staff the higher it will sound.

How long or short — The color of a note (black or white) tells you if it should be played short or long. The black notes in "Mary Had A Little Lamb" are all one beat long (*quarter notes*). The first three white notes in this song are two beats long (*half notes*) and the last note is four beats long (*whole note*).

How the beats are grouped — The two numbers at the beginning of the song (4/4) are called a *time signature*. This time signature tells you that the *beats* in this song are grouped in fours: **1** 2 3 4 **1** 2 3 4 etc. To help you see this grouping, *bar lines* are drawn across the staff to mark each *measure* of four beats. A *double bar* is used to mark the end of the song.

Now here is how "Mary Had A Little Lamb" looks when it is written in musical notes:

MARY HAD A LITTLE LAMB

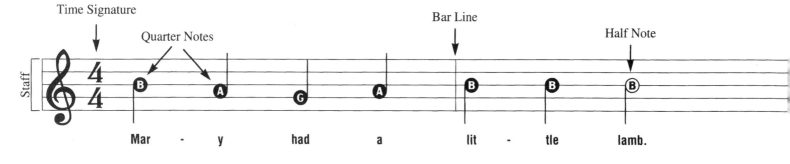

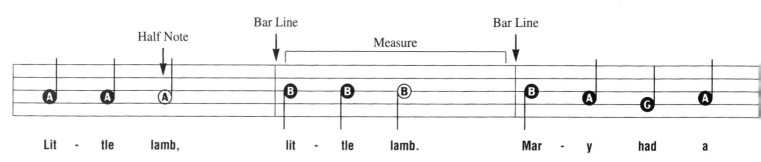

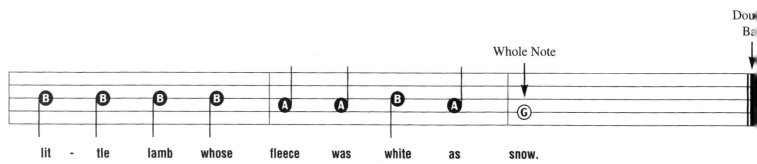

TWO NEW TONES

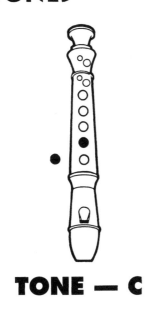

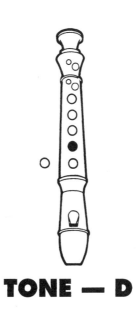

TONE — C   **TONE — D**

AURA LEE

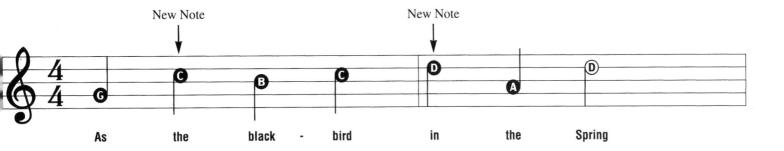

As the black-bird in the Spring

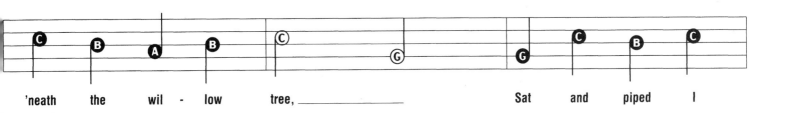

'neath the wil-low tree, _____ Sat and piped I

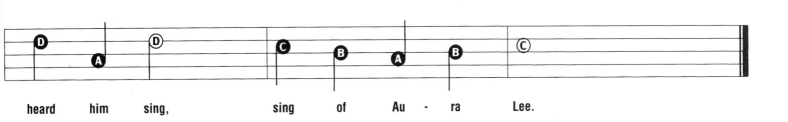

heard him sing, sing of Au-ra Lee.

USING YOUR RIGHT HAND

"Twinkle, Twinkle Little Star" uses the tone E. As you can see from the fingering chart, you will use three fingers of your left hand and two fingers of your right to play this tone. The thumb hole is only half filled in (◑). This means that you should "pinch" the hole with your thumb so that only a small part of the hole is left open. Pinching is done by bending your thumb so that the thumbnail points directly into the recorder leaving the top of the thumb hole open.

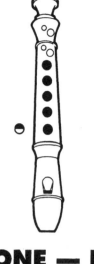

TONE — E

TWINKLE, TWINKLE LITTLE STAR

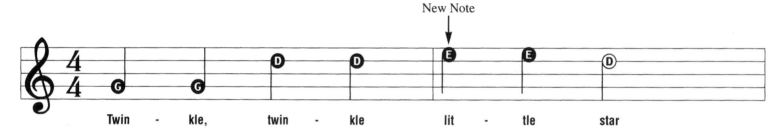

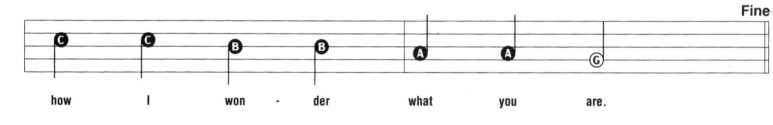

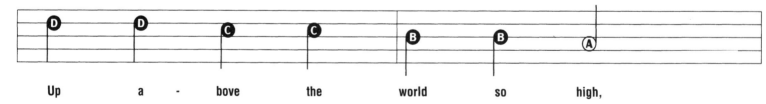

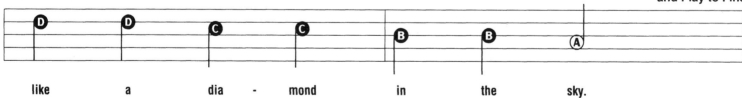

NOTES AND RESTS

In addition to notes that are one, two or four beats long, other values are possible. Also, *rests* are used to indicate when you should *not* play a tone but be silent. The chart on page 7 will help you identify the different notes and rests that are used in this book.

COUNT:	1	&	2	&	3	&	4	&	NUMBER OF BEATS	REST
WHOLE NOTES	o								4	
HALF NOTES									2	
QUARTER NOTES									1	
EIGHTH NOTES					(or)					1/2	
& SIXTEENTHS					(or)					1/4	

DOTTED NOTES ARE 1 1/2 TIMES THE NORMAL LENGTH:

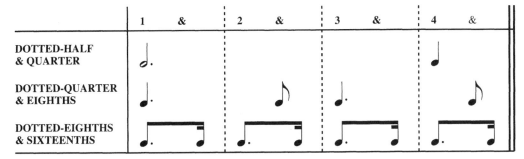

TRIPLETS ARE SPREAD EVENLY ACROSS THE BEATS:

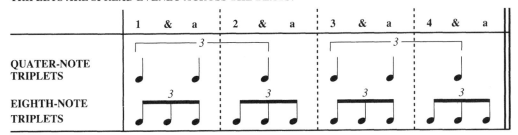

THIS OLD MAN

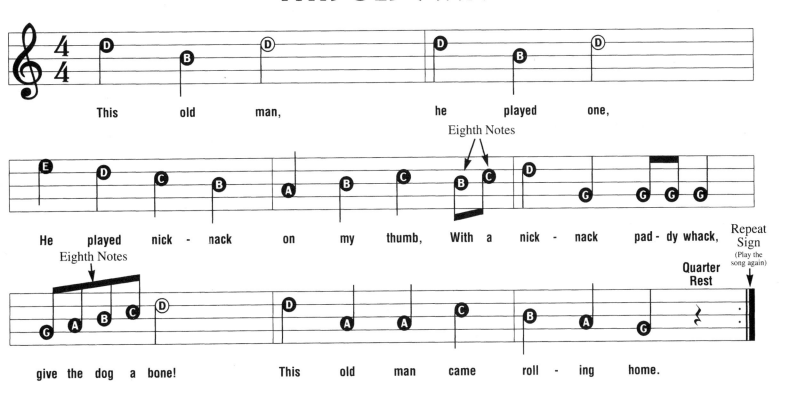

FINGERING CHART

Some tones have two names (C♯/D♭, D♯/E♭). These are called enharmonics. Even though enharmonic notes look different, they will sound the same.

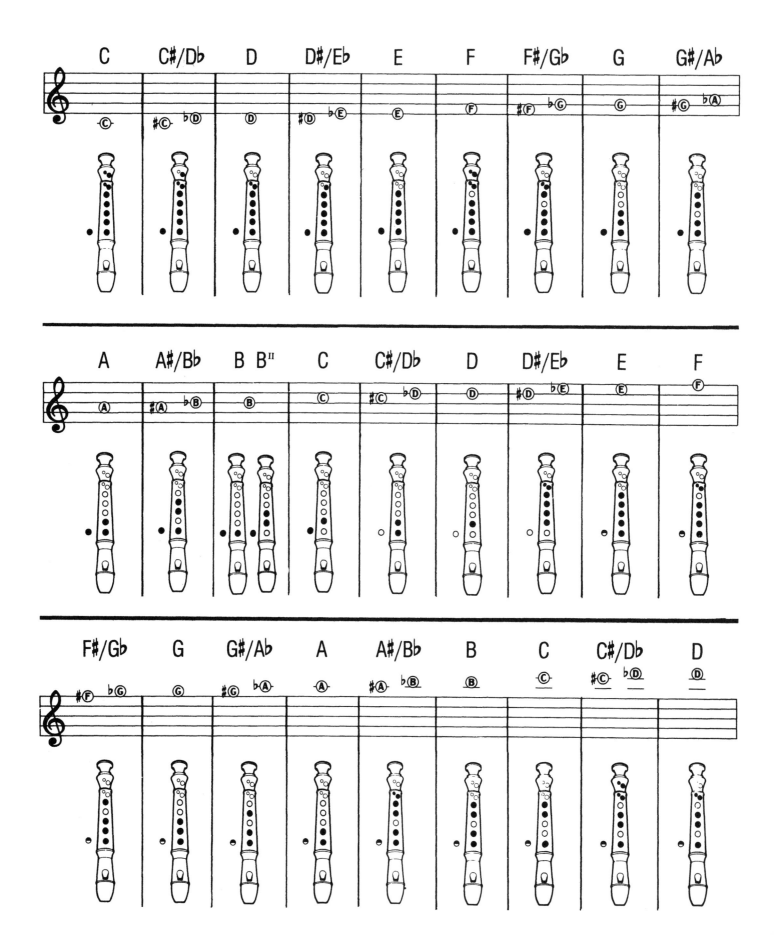

BE KIND TO YOUR WEB-FOOTED FRIENDS

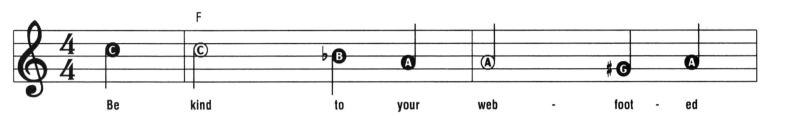

Be kind to your web - foot - ed

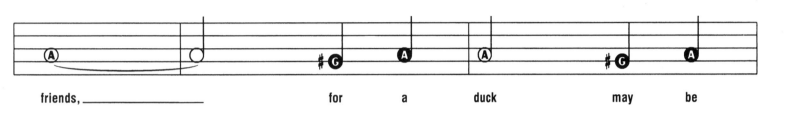

friends,_____ for a duck may be

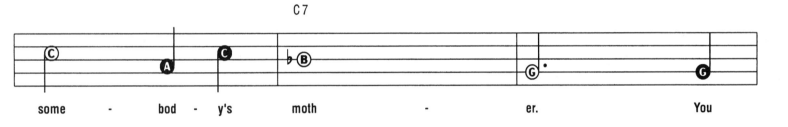

some - bod - y's moth - er. You

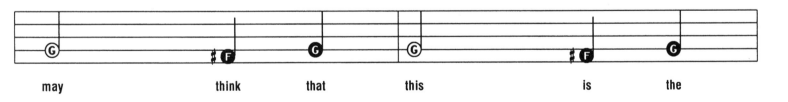

may think that this is the

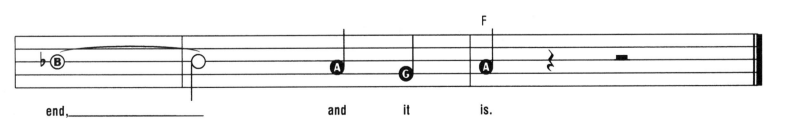

end,_____ and it is.

BILLY BOY

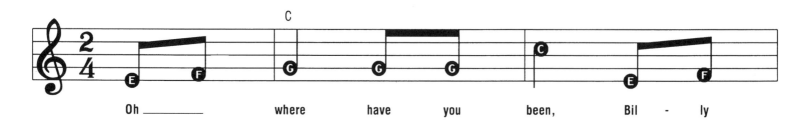

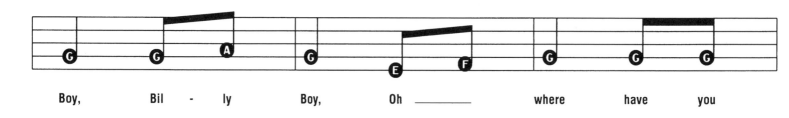

Oh _____ where have you been, Bil - ly

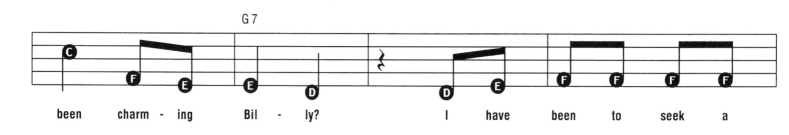

Boy, Bil - ly Boy, Oh _____ where have you

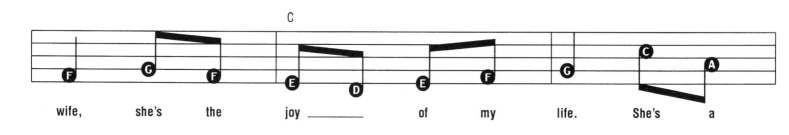

been charm - ing Bil - ly? I have been to seek a

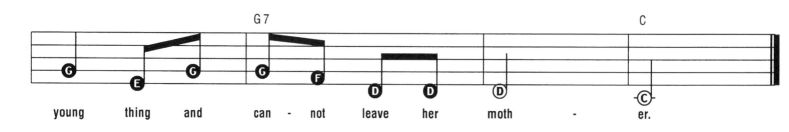

wife, she's the joy _____ of my life. She's a

young thing and can - not leave her moth - er.

CAMPTOWN RACES

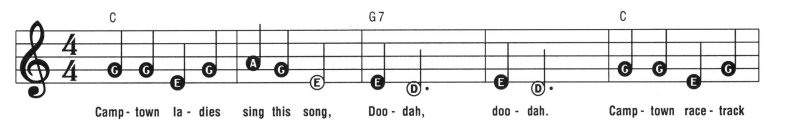

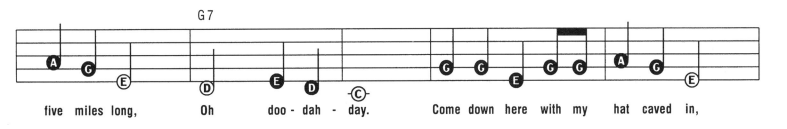

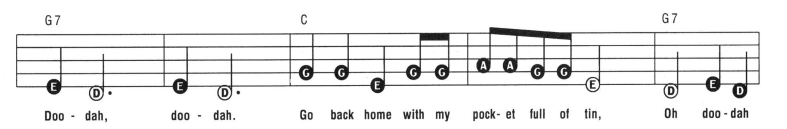

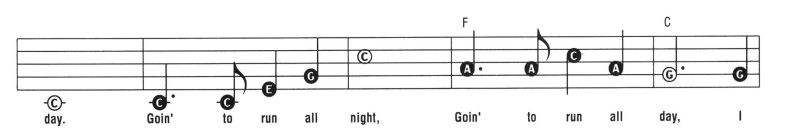

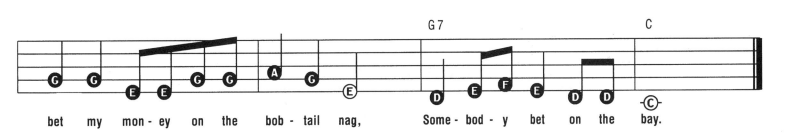

THE FARMER IN THE DELL

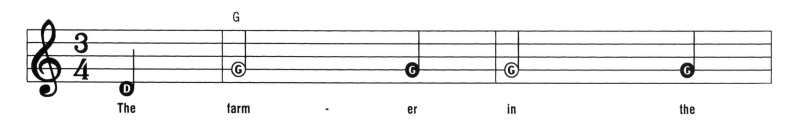

The farm - er in the

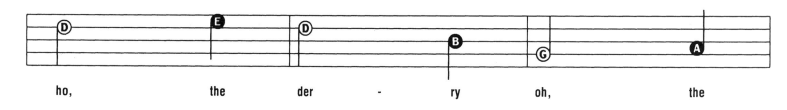

dell, the farm - er

in the dell, Heigh

ho, the der - ry oh, the

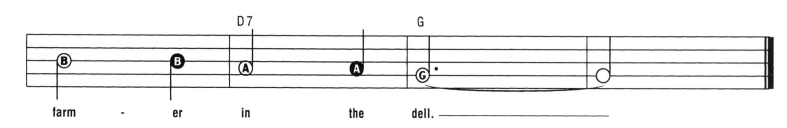

farm - er in the dell.

HICKORY DICKORY DOCK

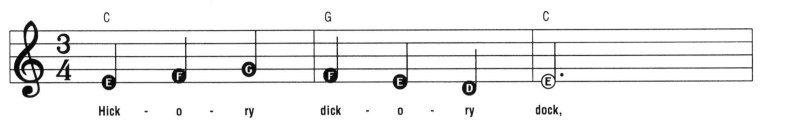

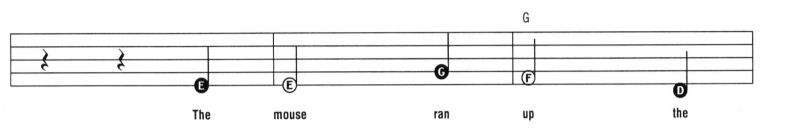

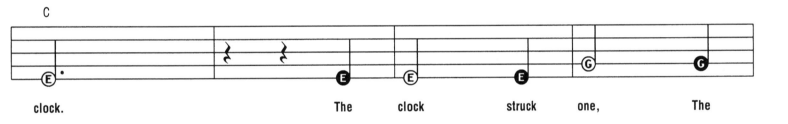

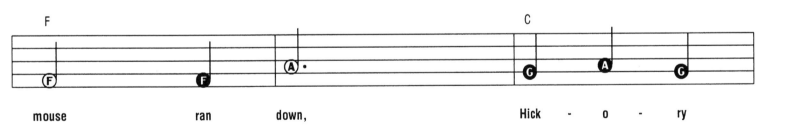

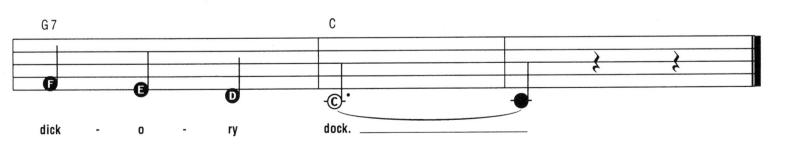

I'VE BEEN WORKING ON THE RAILROAD

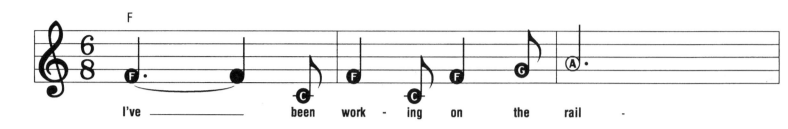

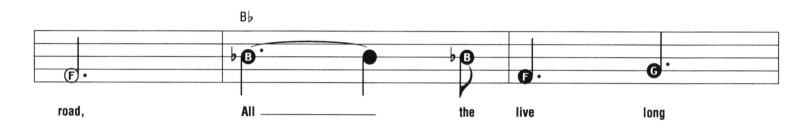

I've ____ been work - ing on the rail -

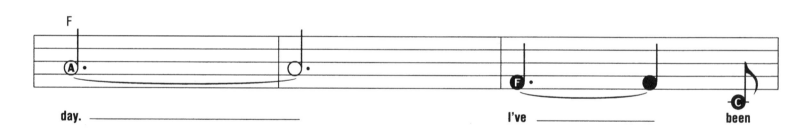

road, All ____ the live long

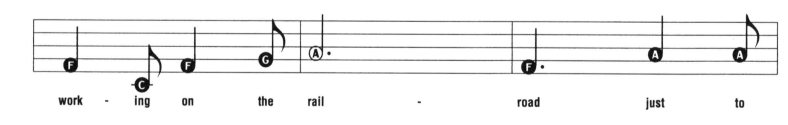

day. ____ I've ____ been

work - ing on the rail - road just to

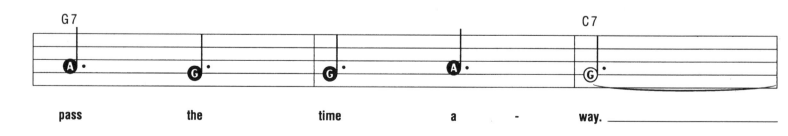

pass the time a - way. ____

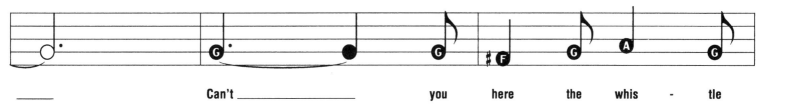

_____ Can't _____ you here the whis - tle

blow - ing? Rise up so

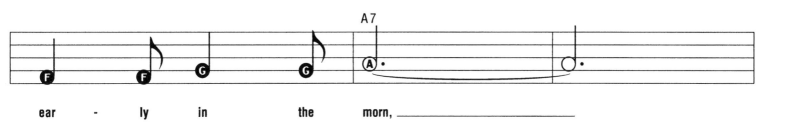

ear - ly in the morn, _____

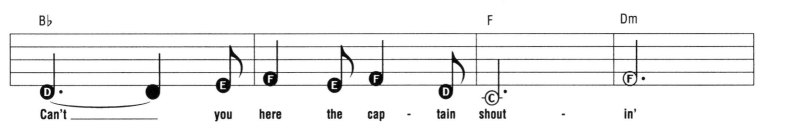

Can't _____ you here the cap - tain shout - in'

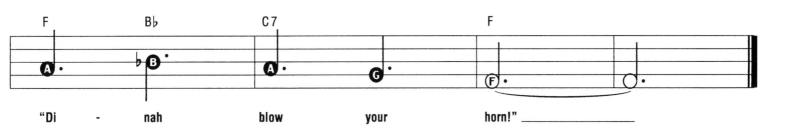

"Di - nah blow your horn!" _____

LONDON BRIDGE

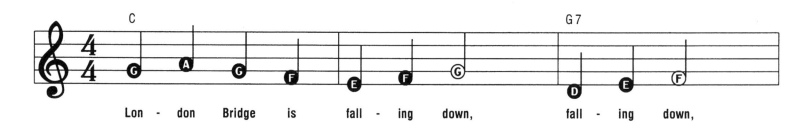

Lon - don Bridge is fall - ing down, fall - ing down,

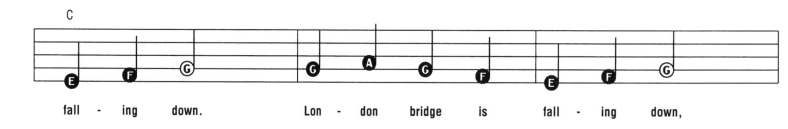

fall - ing down. Lon - don bridge is fall - ing down,

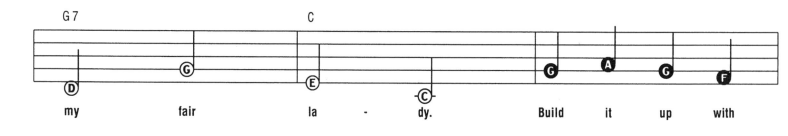

my fair la - dy. Build it up with

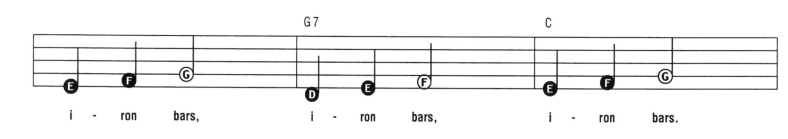

i - ron bars, i - ron bars, i - ron bars.

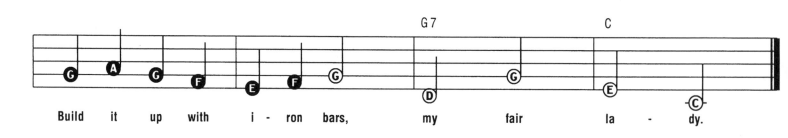

Build it up with i - ron bars, my fair la - dy.

MARY HAD A LITTLE LAMB

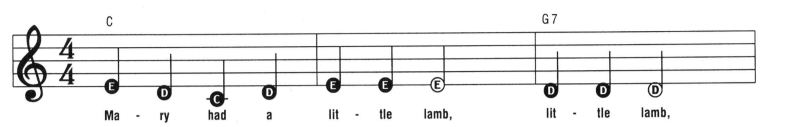

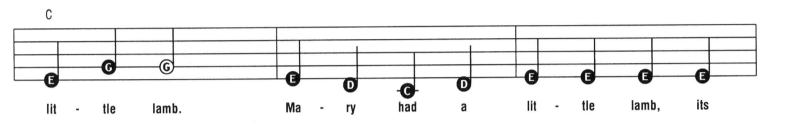

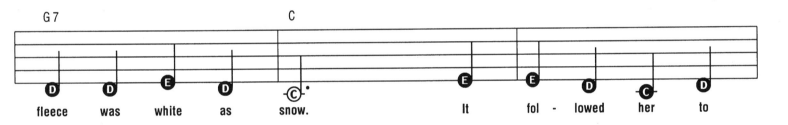

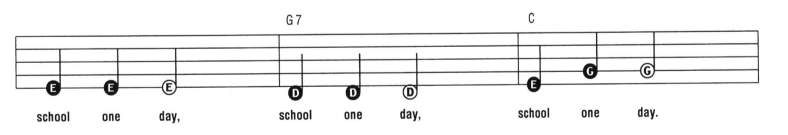

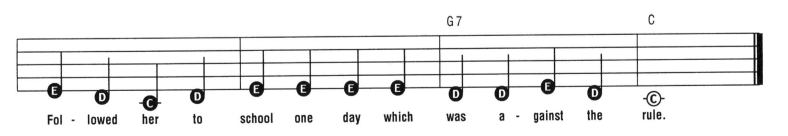

POP! GOES THE WEASEL

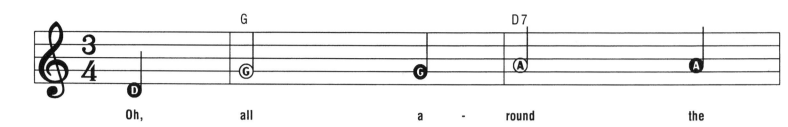

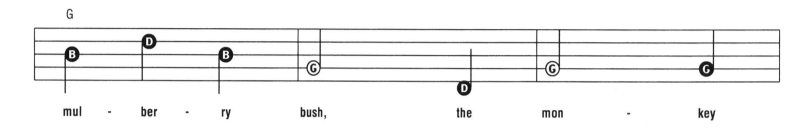

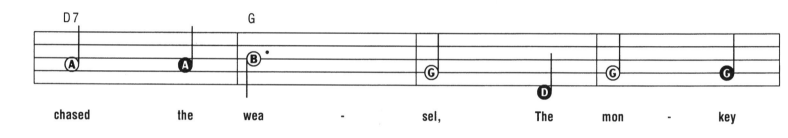

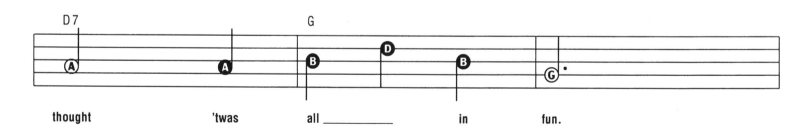

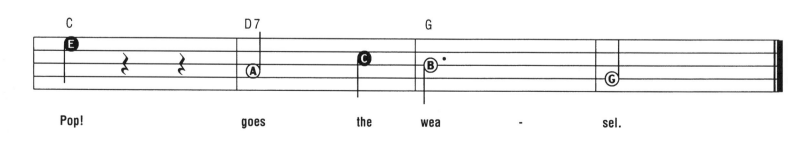

SHE'LL BE COMIN' ROUND THE MOUNTAIN

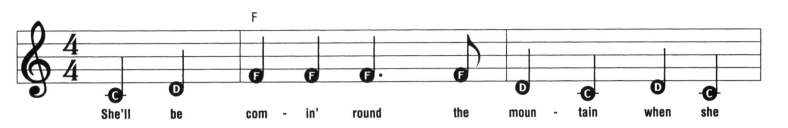

She'll be com - in' round the moun - tain when she

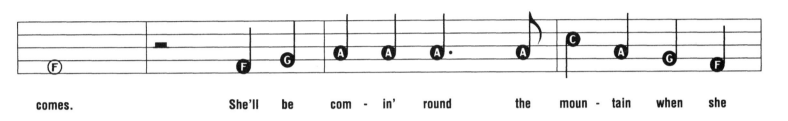

comes. She'll be com - in' round the moun - tain when she

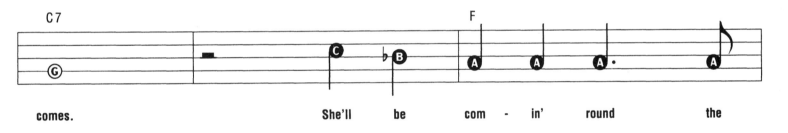

comes. She'll be com - in' round the

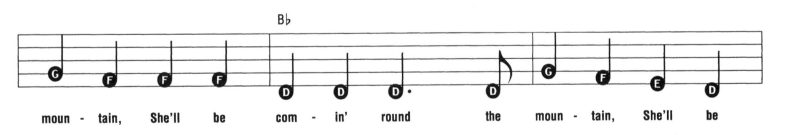

moun - tain, She'll be com - in' round the moun - tain, She'll be

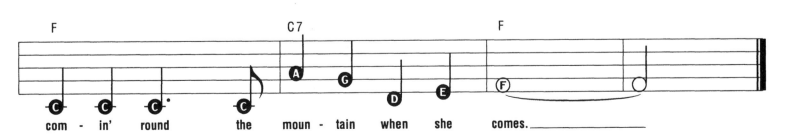

com - in' round the moun - tain when she comes._____

TAKE ME OUT TO THE BALL GAME

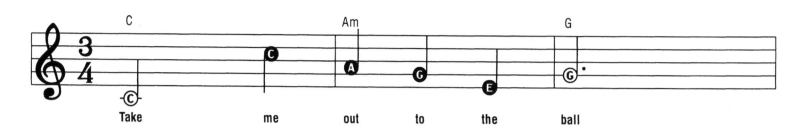

Take   me   out   to   the   ball

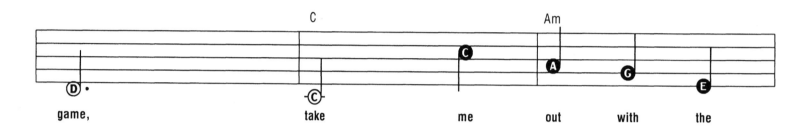

game,   take   me   out   with   the

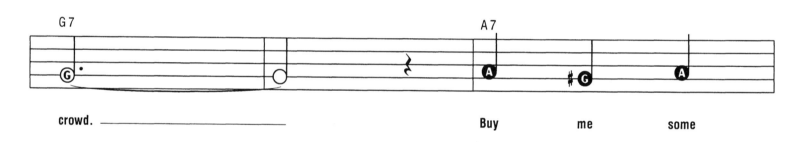

crowd. _____   Buy   me   some

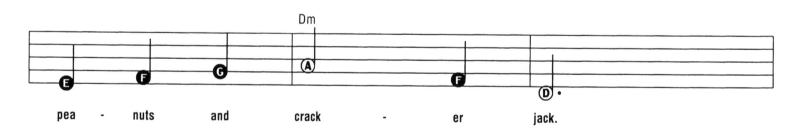

pea - nuts   and   crack - er   jack.

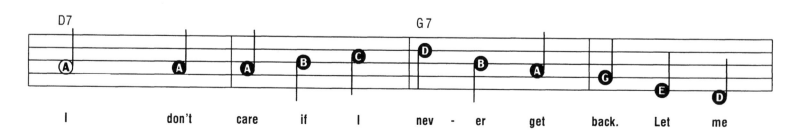

I   don't   care   if   I   nev - er   get   back.   Let   me

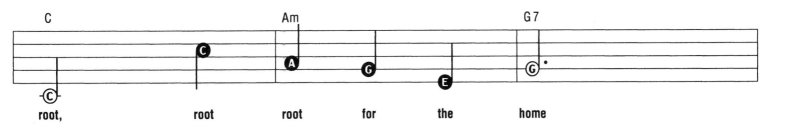

root,   root   root   for   the   home

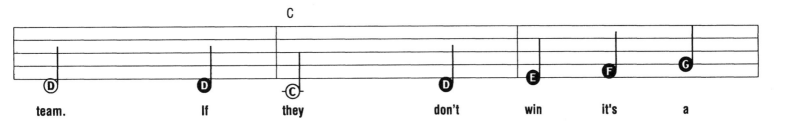

team.   If   they   don't   win   it's   a

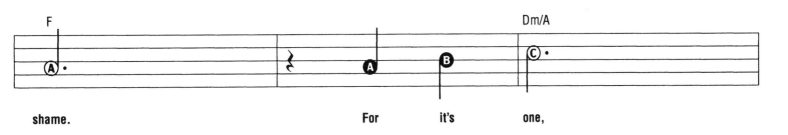

shame.   For   it's   one,

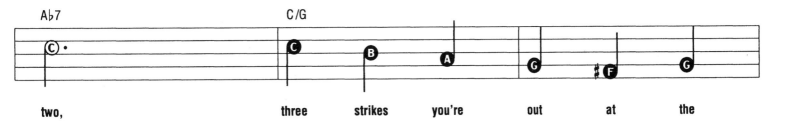

two,   three   strikes   you're   out   at   the

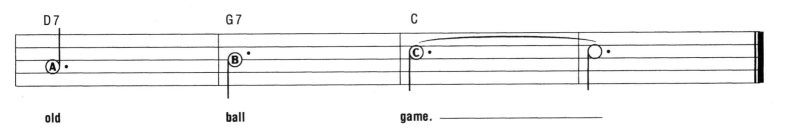

old   ball   game.

THIS OLD MAN

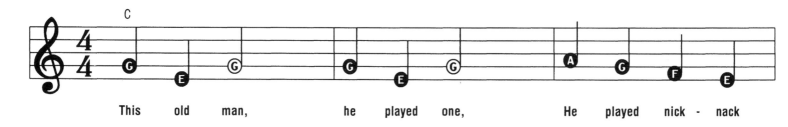

This old man, he played one, He played nick - nack

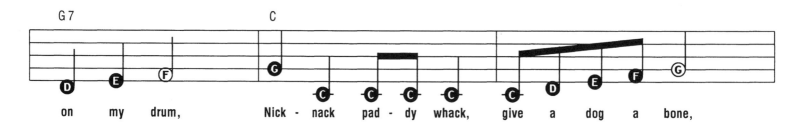

on my drum, Nick - nack pad - dy whack, give a dog a bone,

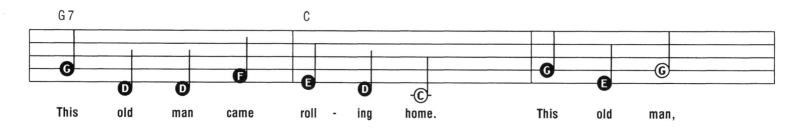

This old man came roll - ing home. This old man,

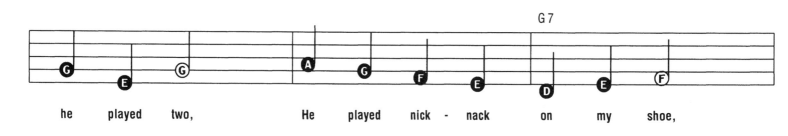

he played two, He played nick - nack on my shoe,

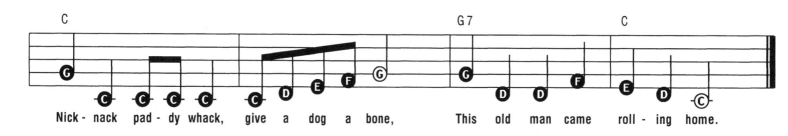

Nick - nack pad - dy whack, give a dog a bone, This old man came roll - ing home.

TWINKLE, TWINKLE, LITTLE STAR

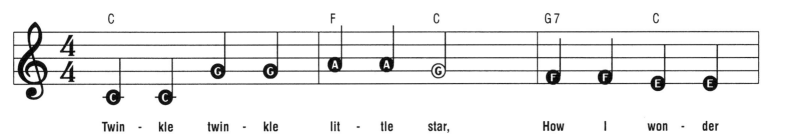

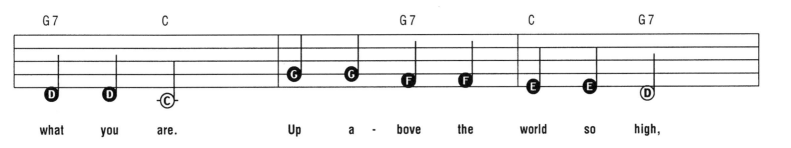

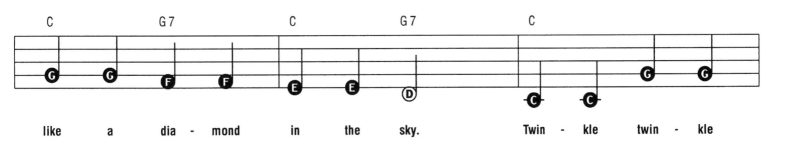

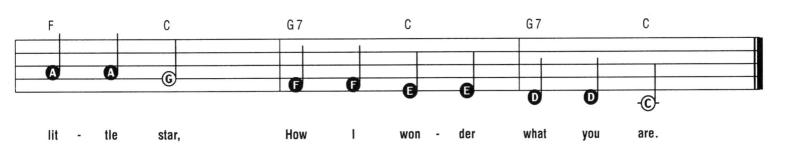

YANKEE DOODLE

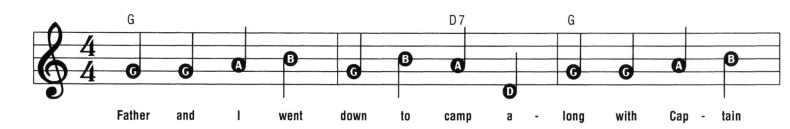

Father and I went down to camp a - long with Cap - tain

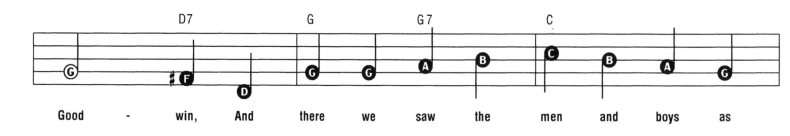

Good - win, And there we saw the men and boys as

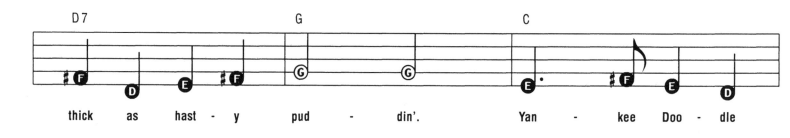

thick as hast - y pud - din'. Yan - kee Doo - dle

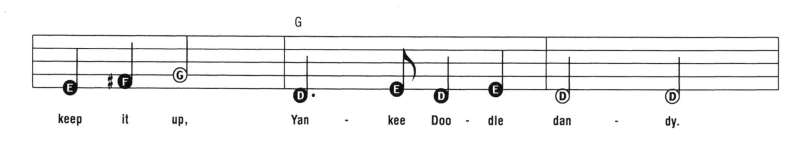

keep it up, Yan - kee Doo - dle dan - dy.

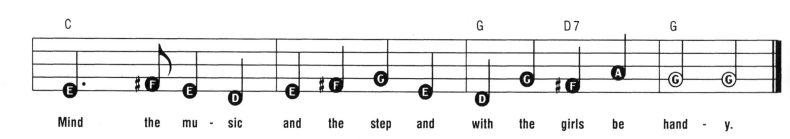

Mind the mu - sic and the step and with the girls be hand - y.